Front cover: Kuwait's Water tanks.
Previous page: Kuwait's Water Towers, a landmark of the country.
This page: Kuwait's magnificent State Mosque.

CONTENTS

BETWEEN THE DESERT AND THE SEA

Along the rim of the shore ran a thin line of houses, built of mud-brick. Around the outskirts of the town, bedu tents would be pitched in the summer months, while along the coast the dhows would come and go, plying their trade or setting off for the oyster beds to the south.

The line of the town stretched along the coast, between the desert and the sea, from close to the modern-day Sheraton Hotel down to where the Kuwait Towers and the Dasman Palace now stand. Inland it stretched a few miles at its broadest point, as far as the First Ring Road, which roughly marks the town's old boundaries.

Travellers' tales and accounts of the 18th and 19th centuries give strong and vivid details of that old town, starkly different from the new in so many ways; and yet the Kuwaiti people and their underlying characteristics have not changed despite many attempts by hostile forces to coerce them into doing so.

From time to time over the years, Kuwait has played a part on the world stage, but always in a quiet, dignified manner, retreating from the limelight again as quickly as possible.

In July 1990, few Westerners could pinpoint exactly where on the map Kuwait stood. One month later, after an unprovoked and audacious invasion from Iraq, everybody knew the answer.

Kuwait lies at the north-western edge of the Arabian Gulf. It covers an area of around 17,820 sq kilometres, has a coastline of 290 kilometres and territorial waters which cover 5,630 sq kilometres and encompass nine islands of varying sizes. The country is bordered by Iraq and by Saudi Arabia. The precise details of its borders with Iraq have now been demarcated by a special United Nations

The sea has played a vital role in Kuwait's development.

Generations of Kuwaitis have been artisans and merchants.

A pearl is scooped from an oyster shell.

Commission, which published its rulings in early 1992. Its findings went a long way towards dispelling any sense of validity in the lingering territorial claims Iraq has made concerning the islands of Bubiyan and Warba, and the Rumailah oilfield. Border markers were put in place by a UN team in October and November 1992.

Kuwait's terrain is predominantly flat, with two areas of high ground, Muttla Ridge, otherwise known as Jal Al Zor, to the north, and the Ahmadi Ridge which runs between the Burgan oilfield and the sea. The first is an impressive sandstone escarpment which fringes the northern shore of Kuwait Bay, but the second, in the south, rises so gradually that it is barely visible except from a distance.

Plants which grow naturally in Kuwait are inevitably those which can thrive in a highly saline soil, and with little water for most of the year. Wildlife abounds or rather, it did prior to the Iraqi invasion and environmental vandalism. Lizards, snakes and small mammals were regularly seen and, around the turn of the century, cheetahs and ostriches roamed the area. However, it is many years since those rarer animals were seen and the Kuwait Institute for Scientific Research is currently investigating which other creatures will have vanished for good as a result of the Gulf War.

Although few species of birds are indigenous to Kuwait, the country lies on the migration route for many, and diverse groups of visitors pass through each year. In the old days, flamingoes regularly paid visits to the mud flats of Kuwait Bay, and Steppe Eagles, Cormorants and Bee Eaters were all spotted in the year before the invasion.

Conditions in Kuwait are harsh. Temperatures as high as 50°C and above are not uncommon in summer, and can plummet below freezing point in winter. The highest recorded temperature was 51°C in July 1978, and the lowest was -6° in January 1964. Little rain falls, but the fluctuation in the exact amount from year to year can be extreme. One year the annual rainfall may be 22 millimetres and the next year it will rise to 352 millimetres. On the whole, the rainfall is spread throughout the cooler months of the year. The most universally disliked weather sees high winds blowing sand and dust into the city. The dust settles like a cloud above the city, and then swirls downwards, occasionally reducing visibility to nil.

Despite all the hardships of life in the region, Kuwait's people have developed a firm sense of independence and national identity which did not

Traditional dress is the norm amongst most Kuwaitis.

desert them during the Occupation. Their roots lie with the desert or the sea or both. The forefathers of today's Kuwaitis were merchants, plying their trade as far as India, Ceylon and Africa; or shipbuilders, crafting the traditional sailing boats which were renowned throughout the region; or pearl divers, spending months of the year at sea working the oyster beds; or bedu, roaming around the desert, seemingly at will, but in fact governed by the seasons and by agreed tribal grazing rights. Or, as the Kuwaitis themselves would have it, they descend from either meat-eaters (bedu) or fish-eaters (seafarers). Through all the changes and rapid developments of the 20th century, Kuwait's people have stayed true to their cultural virtues of hospitality, courtesy and respect.

A modern-day traveller in Kuwait City will be presented with extreme contrasts between the traditional and the modern. This is true of architecture and technology, and of cars and roads, but is most obvious in Kuwait's people. Most Kuwaiti men and women wear traditional costume: dishdasha (long thobe or garment), kefiya (skull cap), agul (black circular ring worn on top of the head-dress to weight it down) and ghutra (cloth head-dress) for the men, and habiya (full length black cloak) or hejab (head-covering) for the women. This often means nothing more than adopting appropriate dress for appropriate occasions, but older women may also choose a burqa or face-covering whenever they are out of the home, and may well keep their hair covered at all times. Women of bedu origin tend to adopt a fuller face-covering, and those who choose to do so are fiercely proud of their right to be protected from the gaze of men.

The mosques call the faithful to prayer five times a day.

Five times each day, the call to prayer rings out across the city, and for many visitors and newcomers to Kuwait this is their first contact with Islam. Kuwait is an Islamic country and is proud to uphold and honour the traditions and teachings of the faith. Ramadan, the holy month in which Muslims fast from sunrise to sunset, is strictly observed but is also a time of family festivity and togetherness. Alcohol and pork products are banned by Islam and by Kuwait.

Kuwait has grown rapidly, with almost 50 years of oil export revenues to sustain it. Since the discovery of oil in 1938, Kuwait has developed an impressive infrastructure of roads, electricity and water-producing installations, schools and hospitals, not to mention some of the world's most advanced oil installations and refineries. It added to its revenues with sound investments, showing a judgement educated by centuries of trading tradition, and dispersed aid to less fortunate Muslim and Arab countries abroad.

Kuwait has been continually threatened in its history, but it was the Iraqi invasion which caused devastation on a national, individual and environmental scale which shocked the world. The Government has been faced with enormous challenges in rebuilding and restructuring the country, and the decade is likely to see still more changes.

Since the restoration of the legitimate government of Kuwait, headed by His Highness the Emir, Sheikh Jaber Al Ahmad Al Jaber Al Sabah, Kuwait has already made massive strides towards democracy, by restoring the Constitution. Elections were held in October 1992 and one of the first resolutions tabled for discussion concerned broadening the electoral franchise, to include women and other groups. Kuwait recognises that its future is with democracy, and has also repealed all laws restricting the press. The coming years will see a phase of vital importance in Kuwait's social and economic development.

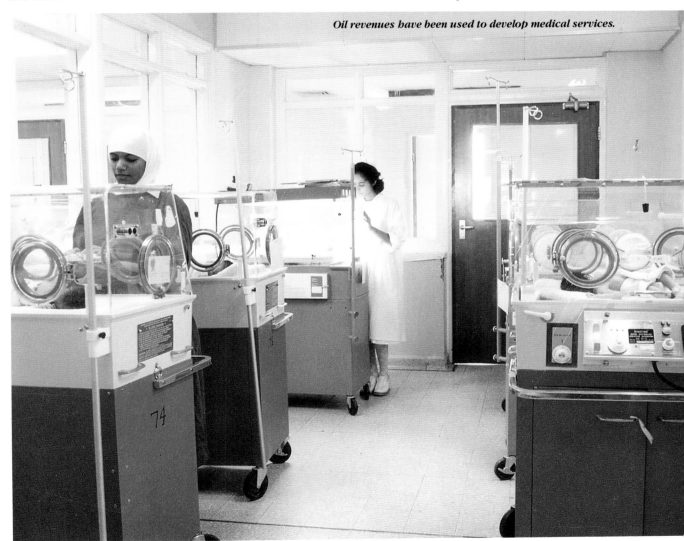

Oil revenues have been used to develop medical services.

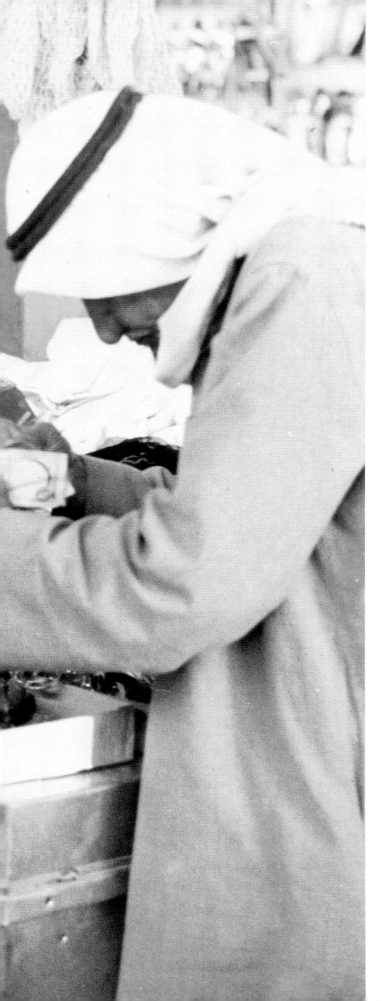

A TRADING NATION

Today Kuwait's regional prominence is due to its oil trade; in fact, commerce has been the key to the area's prosperity and very existence over a period of 4,000 years. Kuwait has had two important advantages in this respect: one of only two good natural harbours in the Gulf (the other was at Bahrain); and a fresh-water supply in its vicinity.

The Ottoman Turks tried to establish control at a series of intervals between the 18th century and the early 20th century, and throughout Kuwait's history there are tales of the schemings of a vast number of varied outsiders, from bedu to the Pasha of Baghdad and major European powers.

Even so, Kuwait has survived the onslaughts, the intrigues, the offensives, and of course, most recently a seven-month Occupation by the Iraqi forces of President Saddam Hussein.

Failika

Since the dawn of recorded time, Kuwait and its islands have been concerned with international trade. History for the country starts between the 2nd and 3rd millennia BC. Archaeological finds on the island of Failika suggest that it was already used as a trading post at the time of the ancient Sumerians and that the first habitation could have been as early as 5,000 years ago, in a Bronze Age civilisation. Some years ago scholars deciphered ancient Sumerian texts which told of the trading power of Dilmun, now known to have been on the island of Bahrain. References to Dilmun have been found on tablets dated around 2,000 BC. Failika, the largest of Kuwait's nine islands, was almost certainly a part of that power, and it is thought that trade links went as far afield as India.

Kuwait's prominence was built on trading and commerce.

13

Gustavo Ferrari

Evidence of Kuwait's origins has been found on Failika.

Dilmun was characterised by red-ridged pottery which has been found in abundance on Failika, together with seals similar to those used in Bahrain. Again, archaeologists discovered that the earlier temple on Failika had been dedicated to Inzak, the guardian deity of Dilmun. Failika is thought to have been a holy island, the centre of religious pilgrimages at that time.

Trading seals show influences that stretch to the Mediterranean and Persia, and suggest that the presence of expatriates in the Kuwait area is by no means a new phenomenon. Failika was so attractive to traders not only because she was a small but well-placed island, but also because she had a fresh-water supply.

There have been numerous digs on Failika, conducted by archaeological teams from Denmark, France, America, and Kuwait. A number of settlements seem to have been occupied again and again at various stages of the island's history. Although she was not central to tales of ancient days, the island was very much a part of the bustle of the past. A ship carrying a block bearing the name of Nebuchadnezzar (a key historical figure who ruled Babylon c.605-562 BC) cast its load there, leaving a stimulating find for archaeologists centuries later, and a dazzling array of countries and empires left their marks on Failika.

The ancient Greeks also knew of Failika, and named it Ikaros after an island in the Aegean. The island was mentioned in contemporary historical documents, particularly in respect of an expedition made by Alexander the Great's Admiral, Nearchus, in 325 BC. The island had a temple, complete with columns, a fort, and a sanctuary. The ancient Greek gods, Apollo and Artemis, were both worshipped there at different times.

Again, archaeological findings indicate that there was a sanctuary on the island before the Greek influence arrived. Written reports stated that the sanctuary was dedicated to a female goddess, whereas material found there suggests a male god, so there is some doubt whether it was the sanctuary referred to, and another may yet be unearthed.

Finds on the island have been prolific. In addition to the numerous buildings, there were terra-cotta figurines, stamp seals, wine jar handles thought to have come from Rhodes, and many coins, including silver tetradrachms from Greece. Failika was clearly an important market place for those who transported exotic goods over a period of more than 2,000 years. Yet all this came to a sudden end. The sanctuary was abandoned and the fortress strengthened, indicating a fear of outsiders. There is no evidence that the island was inhabited after the 1st century AD.

The roots of modern Kuwait

There is a theory that around the end of the 8th century BC, Kuwait was part of the overseas land route through Arabia to Mesopotamia. The years intervening between the end of Failika's function as a trading post and the known history of Kuwait were years of turmoil for Arabia. Commercial activity was disrupted by power after power until Islam spread throughout Arabia in the 7th century AD, eventually travelling as far as Spain and India. The Gulf became a thriving sea route in medieval Islamic times, and again, it is clear that trading links went as far as China. Pearl diving and general trade grew in the area although most of the inhabitants of the region were still nomadic tribes who roamed Arabia at will.

The Portuguese arrived in the Gulf in 1514, and held sway as far north as Bahrain. The Ottoman Turks reached the head of the Gulf overland in 1536, only to be driven out again before the end of the century. And the British, who were determined to maintain control over the Indian Ocean routes were assisting the Persians to recapture Hormuz from the Portuguese as long ago as 1622.

In Kuwait itself, or rather, the part of the Arabian Peninsula which was to become Kuwait, these international wranglings were barely felt. That was to change.

Modern Kuwait has its roots in the past.

Kuwait's bay and anchorages have always been important.

Gustavo Ferrari

Sabah I

For some years Kuwait, with its dry west wind, was a favourite summer resort for the sheikhs of the Bani Khalid tribe who dominated the region. The tribe had held sway in eastern Arabia since the Ottomans were driven out in the 16th century. Based at Al Hasa, they controlled the trade route through the area.

It would appear that at that time, Kuwait was a small fishing village located around a 'kut' or fortress or resort. Travellers of the 18th century also knew the town as Grane, probably an adaptation of the Arabic word 'qarn', which means a small hill. Drinking water had to come from outside the town wall, but the bay was big and there were good anchorages. No one can say for sure exactly when Kuwait was established, but it is thought that it was before the 18th century.

Some time in the 18th century the Utub, a subdivision of the large and powerful Anizah tribe, settled in Kuwait. It is thought that they travelled up from the Qatar area where they had established themselves in the occupations of seafaring and pearl diving. However, historians disagree about their exact origin.

Nominally, the Bani Khalid remained in control of the area, but at some point between 1750 and 1756 Sabah I was established as the Sheikh of Kuwait. He was chosen in the tribal manner for his qualities of generosity and leadership, and his duties were to administer justice and day-to-day affairs in the thriving town. Today Utub families still recall that they were instrumental in choosing the Sabah to oversee the activities of the town while their own forefathers were away on long and often arduous sea journeys.

The town, with its mud houses and wall, controlled an area which went as far north as Jahra, and much further south than the current Kuwait-Saudi border. The sheikh could arrange safe passage for travellers with the bedu tribes in the immediate vicinity of Kuwait and beyond. This was an important source of power as Kuwait sat neatly on the convergence of a number of trade routes. Caravans, sometimes with as many as 5,000 camels could travel from Kuwait to Aleppo in Syria in just 70 days. As well as handling and assisting passing trade, the city itself was growing, with new trades being set up to serve the travellers, meet the needs of the bedu who visited the town suqs (markets), and also to provide the people of Kuwait with goods and services.

Gustavo Ferrari

Heady spices add to the fusion of aromas in the suq.

The Wahhabis

Abu Hakima, a leading historian on Kuwait, has fixed the accession of Abdullah I, the youngest of Sabah I's five sons, at 1762. He ruled until 1812, in a period of Kuwait's history which saw the town growing in regional importance. Once again upheavals outside the borders of the fledgling country were influencing her. Maritime attacks in the Gulf was bothering the British and the Ottomans, and the Bani Khalid tribe was preoccupied with a new threat, the emergence of Sheikh Muhammad bin Abd Al Wahhabi. A militant Islamist, he inspired and led a nomadic group of warriors called the Wahhabis.

Elsewhere, the Persians had conquered Basra from the Ottoman Turks. This meant that all Indian trade with Baghdad, Aleppo, Smyrna and Constantinople was channelled through Kuwait between 1775 and 1779.

An official contract was signed with the British so that the mail from the Gulf to Aleppo was despatched from Kuwait instead of Zubara, in Qatar, between 1775 and 1778. It is clear that Sheikh Abdullah was a shrewd businessman. Kuwait saw a period of prosperity and growth under his rule, and near-contemporary accounts suggest that Abdullah I was "more a father than a governor" to its people.

Sheikh Jaber's reign saw more upheavals in the Arabian region, and more and more scheming from the Ottoman Turks as they tried to bring Kuwait under their control. A British Agent at Basra wrote, "Rather than submit to a Turkish government at Kuwait the people would rather abandon the place."

At that time the Ottoman Turks were apparently collecting statistics to show Kuwait's prosperity was damaging to Basra. They did not like the frequent visits from Britain's merchant steamers.

Boat building is a time-honoured tradition in Kuwait.

Gustavo Ferrari

HH the Emir, great-grandson of Mubarak the Great.

Mubarak the Great

Mubarak was necessarily concerned with foreign policy as his small and prosperous trading town came under continual threat from outsiders, particularly the Ottoman Turks. Mubarak asked for British support, wanting the same relationship and type of treaty that Britain had already signed with the Trucial States (UAE) and Bahrain.

Finally, on 23rd January, 1899, Sheikh Mubarak Al Sabah and the British government signed an agreement, under which the British would provide a measure of protection, but Mubarak was not allowed to receive a representative of any country without the consent of the British, and nor could any Kuwaiti territory be sold to any foreign national or government without their consent.

It was clear that the Ottomans resented the agreement, and at one point an attack on Kuwait seemed imminent. The British Government in India stationed HMS Lapwing off Kuwait to indicate that they would endeavour to prevent this. Further Turkish manoeuvres led to a warning from the British Ambassador to Constantinople. The

Ottomans agreed to back off, and blamed their representative in Basra.

During the recent Iraqi Occupation of Kuwait there were many claims from Saddam Hussein that Kuwait was a British creation, which had previously been under the control of Basra. This is clearly a case of wishful thinking. There is little or no evidence to suggest that Kuwait was ever under the power of the Ottomans, though relations seem to have been friendly immediately prior to the reign of Mubarak.

It is certain however, that outsiders in the region were under the impression that Kuwait came under Turkish control. A German commission at the turn of the century tried to deal directly with Constantinople over land they wished to buy in Kuwait. Mubarak made it clear to them that he was in charge of Kuwait and this was supported by another meeting between the British Ambassador to Constantinople and the Turkish government on 15th April, 1900.

Mubarak was also careful in balancing local tensions. Ibn Saud took residence in Kuwait in 1897, and received help from Mubarak in his military endeavours to win control of Najd, now in Saudi Arabia. As with any factional wranglings, a friend of one side, by implication, is inevitably an enemy of the other, and through helping Ibn Saud, Mubarak and Kuwait then had to contend against Ibn Rashid, another key figure in the power struggles which led to the foundation of modern Saudi Arabia. Mubarak marched against Ibn Rashid and was victorious, which resulted in Ibn Saud's son being appointed governor of Riyadh.

The Turks used the conflict as a springboard for yet another attempt to take control, obligingly suggesting that they place a garrison in Kuwait, in order to protect it. Mubarak politely declined their offer.

However, Ibn Rashid's attempt to take control of the region led to thousands of bedu and their livestock coming to Kuwait Town for protection, erecting a huge camp of camel hair tents on the outskirts. The British were eventually persuaded to bring their gunboats to Kuwait in readiness for an attack.

By November 1901 Ibn Rashid was on the frontier, and the ruler of Basra was trying to get Mubarak to swear loyalty to the Sultan of Turkey, which would of course have entailed the loss of independence. This brought further diplomatic protests from the British and the Turks sent a warship to Kuwait with an ultimatum. The British made a display of strength to support Mubarak, Ibn Rashid backed down, and the Turks changed their tactics, gradually occupying Um Qasr and Bubiyan in 1902 in a policy of gradual encroachment on Kuwaiti territory which the United Nations Commission discovered had been emulated by modern-day Iraq.

As foreign powers started to pay more and more attention to the power struggles going on in what was to become Saudi Arabia, the pressure on Kuwait reduced. It could be said that Mubarak the Great was the first ruler of Kuwait to have had an active foreign policy which went further than mere reaction to outside events.

In accounts of Mubarak's rule, he is portrayed as a highly competent ruler and it was said that tribal affairs were so well managed during his reign that opposition to his wishes was seldom heard of. Mubarak died in 1915. In 1914 the population of the town was 35,000 people. The town consisted of 3,000 houses, 500 shops, and three schools. There were around 500 boats engaged in pearl-fishing and 30 or 40 larger vessels sailing to India and Africa. There were as many as 300 boat builders, working with timber imported from India.

The beautiful lines of the State Mosque are reflected in the glass exterior of the Stock Exchange.

Gustavo Ferrari

The cultured pearl trade hit Kuwait's pearl divers badly.

The Battle of the Red Fort

In 1920, Sheikh Salem, who had come to the throne a few years earlier, was confronted by an Ikhwan attack on Jahra, at the Qasr Al Ahmar (Red Fort). Until 2nd August, 1990 this was the most serious battle in Kuwait's history. With limited support from the British, Sheikh Salem's forces were victorious.

Salem died in 1921 to be succeeded by Ahmad Al Jaber. A time of prosperity followed which saw both shipbuilding and pearling industries thriving. In 1922 came the first attempt to set internationally recognised boundaries for Kuwait, at the Uqair conference. Oil had been found in Persia and the region was beginning to take on a new importance for foreign powers.

But even while Kuwait was negotiating with the various oil concerns, her economy was badly hit, first by a Saudi blockade and embargo which continued till 1938, and by the rise of the Japanese cultured pearl industry. This was a very difficult period for Kuwait's economy as most families were involved in trade or pearling.

Kuwait Oil Company

In 1934 the Kuwait Oil company (KOC) was formed as a joint venture between the Anglo-Persian Oil Company and the Gulf Oil Company which was later to become British Petroleum (BP). Exclusive exploration rights were granted to KOC, but nobody had any idea whether or not they would strike oil, or how much they would find if they did.

The first strike was at Burgan in 1938, and others followed. World War II stopped either drilling or export, but there was oil aplenty underground, so the town of Ahmadi was created to cope with the fledgling industry, and was named after the ruler.

In June 1946 Sheikh Ahmad inaugurated the first oil terminal, sending Kuwait's first export shipment of crude oil on its way.

After his death in 1950 Sheikh Abdullah Salem Al Sabah became the ruler. Under his rule Kuwait grew and changed as the oil revenues, far exceeding anything that had ever been dreamt of, began to pour in. Achievements in the fields of oil, electricity, water, housing, schools and hospitals abounded, gradually changing the face of modern Kuwait. Many of the old properties between Safat Square and the Seif Palace were destroyed at this time as the old was shunned in favour of the new.

It was also during Sheikh Abdullah's rule that Kuwait achieved total independence in 1961. Its Constitution was ratified in November 1962 and became valid in January 1963. Kuwait joined the Arab League in 1961 and became a member of the United Nations in 1963.

By the time he died, in 1965, Abdullah had taken Kuwait from a primitive backwater town to a highly modern and flourishing state. He was succeeded by Sheikh Sabah Al Salem, whose reign saw 13 years of overwhelming prosperity and growth. In 1975 the government took full ownership of KOC, and showed that it was both capable of control and determined to manage its own affairs without international interference.

In 1981 the Arab Gulf Co-operation Council, a six-state alliance between Bahrain, Kuwait, Oman, Qatar, Saudi Arabia and the UAE was formed, with the intention of placing the affairs and security of the region under local, not international control.

Oil wealth has changed the course of Kuwait's history.

THE OLD WAYS

Some of what is known about the lifestyles of the earlier inhabitants of Kuwait City comes through travellers' tales and books of the time. Other information has been handed down within families, and still more is current memory — after all, there are those alive today who were themselves pearl-divers or sea-captains, and who remember Kuwait before oil was even thought of.

Kuwait's oldest residents at the time of writing are more than 110 years old, and were born long before the reign of Mubarak the Great.

These old people have seen almost unfathomable change during their lives. Kuwait has changed even in 10 years, the alterations that have taken place in the life-span of a 70-year-old are legion. Their memories of the desert and of the sea are vital to Kuwait's sense of identity as a unique state with a culture built on hardships and years of austerity.

Visitors today can be blinded by the sheer wealth around them, but it should not be forgotten that it took overwhelming hard work and effort merely to survive, let alone prosper in those days. Kuwait was not built on oil wealth alone, but on the efforts and achievements of the previous generations of Kuwaitis.

Nor should visitors forget the immense achievements of those who survived the Occupation, a time of crisis, pain and despair.

Life was hard and conditions were harsh when the old men and women of today were children. The first organised medical facilities came to Kuwait only in 1911. The infant mortality rate was as high as 50 per cent in certain sections of the society, and epidemics hit the town again and again, notching up a high death toll. In the smallpox epidemic of 1932 4,000 people died in the first 10 days alone.

Old traditions continue today, side by side with the new.

Water was a valuable commodity and a luxury. At the beginning of the century the wells on the perimeters of the town were insufficient for its needs and water had to be transported in from Basra by dhow. There was no such thing as air conditioning, and townsman and bedu alike had to learn to survive the rigours of one of the toughest climates on earth.

Travellers' tales

A surprising number of travellers passed through Kuwait and wrote about their experiences in the 18th and 19th centuries. Their accounts help us to assess the development, growth and prosperity of the town.

One of the first was Corsten Niebuhr, a Dane, who made one of the earliest maps showing Kuwait. In 1764 he reckoned the population of Kuwait to be around 10,000, with a fleet of 800 small boats working the pearl beds. He tells us that when Kuwait was threatened by outsiders in those days everyone would take up their belongings and move to Failika until the threat receded.

Buckingham, an Englishman who was travelling through in 1816, described the populace of Kuwait as "mostly merchants, brave and freedom-loving" and the town as a "port of some importance".

In 1831, the traveller Stocqueler, who has provided an important source for historians, recorded that Kuwait town had 4,000 inhabitants, and Captain Hennel, the British resident in the Gulf, wrote in 1841 that Kuwait was "wanting in almost every advantage except its harbour". By 1863, Colonel Pelly was describing Kuwait as a compact town with 15,000 inhabitants. Pelly went on to write a book, *A Journey to Riyadh in Central Arabia* describing his experiences, and recalls in detail a stay with Sheikh Yusef ben Badr of the Al Badr family, who at that time was a sprightly old man of 72.

Lorimer's *Gazeteer of the Gulf* another excellent source for historians, describes daily life in the town as well as the nature of trade and of historical events and conflicts. A strong picture emerges of an independent and thriving community, managing to survive despite the harsh conditions.

Life in the town

The town had a wall with five gates, to protect it from unfriendly outsiders. This ran roughly along where the First Ring Road is today. Yet even though

A replica of one of the old gates of Kuwait which provided entry to the town for the bedu and travellers.

the desert and its people were shut out at night, a considerable amount of trade was done with the bedu tribes who would come close to its walls during the summer, partly so that they could water their flocks from the wells nearby, but also so that they could buy from the merchants of the town the goods they could not make themselves. They would need these during the autumn, winter and spring, when they would move far into the desert. Although townsfolk and desert bedu lived such vastly different lives they were mutually dependent on each other.

Inside the town, life continued at a slow pace. Many of the men were away for most of the year, either on the pearling boats, or else travelling to India and beyond for trade. Others were involved in fishing and shipbuilding.

The heart of the town was Safat Square, which still exists, albeit in a form which ancestors of today's Kuwaitis would be unlikely to recognise. The townsfolk would gather there to watch traditional dancing and to celebrate such special occasions as the Eid Al Fitr. The gentle hill of the town sloped downwards from the square to the sea front, where the dhows, booms and smaller boats would be anchored. The wealthier families would live along the sea front, and behind them the closely knit, mud-brick houses and streets would intertwine haphazardly.

There were a number of suqs. The major one of these was close to Safat, running down to the shore, and others would be held near to the town gates, particularly those specialising in providing goods required by the bedu. There were also coffee

Safat Square, once the centre of Kuwait's social gatherings.

A 'hadra' trap — fish are stranded at low tide.

houses in the suqs, where the men who were not otherwise occupied would go to drink coffee, smoke the hubble bubble or nargeilah pipe, and to play board games. Often the coffee house would be little more than a row of benches in a lane.

In 1914 the population was 35,000. The town had 3,000 houses, 500 shops, three caravanserais, six coffee houses, three schools, and numerous warehouses and stores. By 1930 the population had risen to 60,000.

Fishing was a main source of food, and the waters of Kuwait provided fish and prawns in abundance. In addition to the usual methods of fishing by casting nets from a boat, Kuwait had two types of fish trap, which again, are still used to this day. These were called 'gargoor' and 'hadra'.

'Gargoor' is a large portable trap similar to a huge lobster pot. Once the fish swim in through a central funnel they are unable to manoeuvre out again before the fishermen haul it up. 'Hadra' is a complicated maze of sticks in shallow water. Again, there is a definite path inwards, which the fish will not be able to follow out again, particularly as the tide recedes over the entrance. The fish are driven inwards and can finally be picked up from the centre chamber by hand at low tide. There are still a number of these dotted along the shore, in Abu Halifa, Salmiyah and near the British Embassy building.

Kuwait also had a flourishing boat building industry. Ten different kinds of ship and boat were built by craftsmen, many of whom originally came from Bahrain. The materials, particularly the teak wood, were brought in from India. At the beginning of this century there were an estimated 300 boat builders working in Kuwait. Some dhows are still built in Kuwait, but the industry has declined almost to nothing.

'Gargoor' fish traps aboard a dhow before being dropped in Kuwait Bay.

Family life early in the 20th century

The family is and always has been one of the most important institutions of Kuwaiti society. It has been remarked that Kuwait doesn't have political parties, but has families instead. Although this is a gross over-simplification, it nevertheless contains an element of truth. Many of the families who were part of that original Utub division are still prominent in Kuwait today. These families include the Al Badr family, who once lived at the Bayt Al Badr (now part of the National Museum Complex on the Gulf Road); the Al Qatami family, who were primarily seafarers and merchant traders; and the prominent international businessmen of today, the Al Khaleds, the Al Saqrs, the Al Ghanim, and so on.

Family has a vital role in the day-to-day life of an individual, and this can be seen from the structure of Kuwaiti names. If a man gives his name as Badr Khalifa Ahmed Al Mutair he is not only identifying himself but is also pinpointing his genealogy precisely and accurately. Khalifa is the name of his father, and Ahmed the name of his grandfather. Mutair is his tribe. This system is as true today as it was a hundred years ago and more.

Marriage took place early, and first rights to marrying a girl went to the male cousin on the father's side. Once a suitable arrangement was planned, the women of both families would meet first, unofficially, and then, if all went well, the men of the groom's family would visit the men of the bride's family to ask for her hand in marriage. There are many family proverbs which stress the importance of marrying within the clan, and most are concerned with the need to keep property within the family. If another man wished to marry a girl it would be considered necessary for him to seek her cousin's permission.

A house would be constructed so that the women could come and go without ever being seen by visitors, and often there would be separate courtyards for the men and for the family. Segregation was carefully observed and women and men led lives which were almost completely separate and different.

Women's lives were totally absorbed in looking after the family. Marriage and childbirth were seen

Kuwaitis are proud of their heritage and traditions, passing them down from generation to generation.

Sadu weavings: a bedu woman works on a tent.

as a woman's main function in life and she would work from first light to dusk, fetching water from the water-seller, baking bread, and preparing the often complicated dishes which formed the Kuwaiti diet at that time, generally consisting of bread, rice, dates, some vegetables and occasionally fish. The rest of her time would be spent weaving rugs and sewing clothes.

Not only did she work hard, but she would also be alone with her children for most of the year. For that reason the companionship of other women was important and they would visit each other in their houses, taking their work along with them.

Children had little or no formal education other than in the teachings of the Koran, and for the most part were allowed to run wild along the shores of Kuwait. There are stories of large gangs of children from different areas who would fight, and even stories of strangers being unceremoniously dumped in the sea by the urchins. They would also fish by catching poisonous crabs and grinding them up. The crushed crustacean would then be sprinkled on the sand just below the tide mark, for the fish to eat and then die. This sounds a little far-fetched but it seems that it worked, and that women would also fish in this way while the menfolk were at sea.

Leisure time was a rare luxury, and would usually come at religious holidays such as the Eid Al Fitr and the Eid Al Adha. There would be horse and camel races and traditional dances to watch, and new clothes to parade in, especially if the men were just back from sea.

Sailing by dhow to India

In 1914 Kuwait had 500 pearl-diving crews, and 30 to 40 larger vessels sailing to India and Africa. These merchants and their crews were often away from home as long as the pearl divers, and sometimes for longer. Abdullah Al Badr, a member of one of the leading families in Kuwait, recalls that his family's trading activities could see a dhow captain and crew away from home for many months. Perhaps the first stop would be Basra where a dhow would load dates for India, he explains. Once the dhow arrived at India to deliver its cargo, it would then find another cargo, perhaps teak, destined for another port, such as Zanzibar. At Zanzibar they would load another local cargo. His own family was once famous for breeding and exporting horses to Bombay.

The journeys, though lucrative, could often be hazardous. There are many tales of shipwreck in shark-infested waters, and of heroism and bravery. The dhows would also go to and from Basra where they would pick up a cargo of fresh water.

In the middle of the 19th century George Brucks prepared a report for the Indian Navy which detailed the activities in the various Gulf ports. According to this report, Kuwait traded in wheat, coffee and Indian goods and had 15 large vessels with a tonnage averaging between 100 and 400 tonnes and 20 smaller cargo ships as well as numerous other vessels. Goods imported by Kuwait at this time were listed as cloth, rice, sugar, wood, spices and cotton, as well as items available from neighbouring countries. Exports included pearls, ghee and horses.

The merchant group was already well-versed in international commerce and trade long before the discovery of oil. There have been many portraits of Kuwait which show the country as a primitive backwater thrust suddenly into the 20th century, but in fact that merchant class was already well-equipped to take advantage of their new and astronomical wealth. Instead of trading primarily with India and Africa, as they had before, when oil

Kuwait was renowned for her fine horses.

Powerboat racing is now a popular sport in Kuwait.

was discovered they turned their attention to America, Britain, Europe and the rest of the world, building on the expertise and knowledge of their fathers.

It is easy to lose sight of the humanity of these men who plied the trade routes, looking only at the hardships and overlooking the lighter moments. Khalifa Al Qatami, who comes from a fine old seafaring family, is today a well-known adept at one of Kuwait's most popular sports, powerboat racing. He tells of races held between dhows long ago, the spirit of competition providing the crews with energy to go beyond simple endeavour.

One time, he says, a member of the Qatami family was challenged by the master of another vessel to beat him to Bombay; the first one into Bombay harbour would win the race. However, his dhow was delayed, and set off a full week after the first dhow.

The crew tried everything they could to make up lost time, keeping full sail, and eventually tossing things overboard to make the dhow lighter. Apparently some or all of the cargo was also cast overboard in an attempt to make up time.

When they entered Bombay harbour they were dismayed to find that there was no other Kuwaiti dhow in sight; their opponents must have come and gone. When they questioned the harbour master he told them he hadn't seen another Kuwaiti vessel for days. They were disappointed that all their effort had been for nothing, but realised that, with a week's delay before sailing, they had been up against unbeatable odds. However, it was two whole days later that the other dhow actually arrived!

While they waited for cargoes, crews would also engage in rowing races in the harbour, says Al Qatami, adding that races occasionally took place from Basra to Kuwait, a much shorter distance than Kuwait to Bombay. A relative of his, racing neck and neck against a rival dhow, tried to inch forward at the finishing point by keeping full sail as the dhow came into harbour. It took four anchors to stop the boat, but not before the dhow, and several boats already in the harbour were badly damaged. Such hot-headed racing was frowned upon, but places the activities of the youngsters of today neatly in context.

The spirit of competition has always existed between dhow crews.

Pearl diving

Crews of men between 15 and 50 years of age would head for the oyster beds off Bahrain and Qatar each year. Before World War I, 700 Kuwaiti boats were working the beds, providing work for between 10,000 and 15,000 men. The value of pearl exports at the turn of the century was £1.43 million sterling, with a further £30,439 coming from the export of mother-of-pearl.

The diving season would run from the middle of May to the end of September, when sea conditions would begin to deteriorate. Boats would travel as far as Sri Lanka in order to take advantage of the best pearl oyster beds, and principal markets were in Bombay and Bahrain.

The vessels were owned by individual merchants or companies who would pay the divers a portion of the profits at the end of the voyage. Of course, if the voyage was not fruitful, there would be little cash to share, and the divers needed to be able to maintain their families during their absence.

Consequently a system developed whereby the merchant would lend the diver money at the start of the trip so that this could be given to his family. The men would then repay the loan when they received their share of the season's profits. If the season was poor then debts would mount up. Other divers were self-employed and were transported on the ships in exchange for a portion of their profits, which they paid to the owner at the end of the trip. Thus good years saw plenty and comfort for the pearl-diving community but bad years brought great hardship. It was certainly a tough way of making a living, necessitating total fitness and long periods away from home.

There were also many dangers to be encountered on the voyage, from sharks and poisonous sea snakes to storms and sudden squalls. In 1871 many diving ships were sunk by a massive hurricane between Oman and India. This was called the Al Taba'ah disaster. It is small wonder that the women would wait on the shore in eagerness to see their husbands as soon as the vessel came close to shore.

The lateen-rigged craft faced many dangers at sea.

Bedu in the desert

The bedu led a life which was dominated by the rhythms of the seasons, by dawn and by dusk, and by the control of the tribe. Raiding parties would go out on skirmishes against other tribes, and the bedu code of honour was precise about the conduct to be followed on such trips, and about what could and could not be stolen. For example, it was acceptable to take a neighbour's camel, but not if it was a female in calf. A bedu family's wealth would be measured by the size of his flocks of goats, sheep, horses, and most importantly, camels. His grazing rights would depend on his tribe. A 'dira', or grazing area, for one tribe could cover an area as large as 56,000 square kilometres, extending beyond national boundaries.

In summer the bedu would move in to be near the wells surrounding Kuwait, and would stay within walking distance. They would also use the time to shop for those items they could not make themselves. The year 1940 was especially harsh and hot, and the wells at Jahra, Subaihiya and Subaih, nowadays swallowed by the sprawl of modern Kuwait, were the only hope for the bedu. Violet Dickson, who lived in Kuwait for over 60 years and was a prolific writer, reported having seen over 200 tents clustered around the Jahra well that year.

In winter they could roam as far as they liked. Plants would grow rapidly in spring, particularly after rainfall, providing good grazing for the animals, and rain would tend to lie on the baked ground for a long period of time, providing water. The bedu also used animals known to need little water — camels of course, but also sheep, goats and horses.

Traditionally they would live in the 'bayt al shar' (literally, the house of hair), which was woven by the women out of camel hair. The women would pitch the tent and have very definite living areas of their own (as did their sisters in the towns) away from the quarters of the men.

A traditional craft of major importance was sadu weaving, consisting of geometric designs woven in hand-dyed and spun, coloured wool. The loom consisted of a number of sticks anchored by stones, and the whole affair could be rolled up and moved when the tribe was in transit, without damaging the work in progress. The tent itself would be woven in this way, as indeed would its brightly coloured and decorative side flaps, as well as attractive cushions and camel saddle bags which provided a touch of comfort.

Sheep remain an important sign of a bedu family's wealth.

Geometric designs are worked in hand-spun wool.

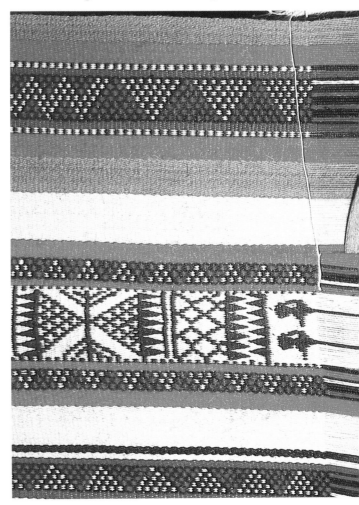

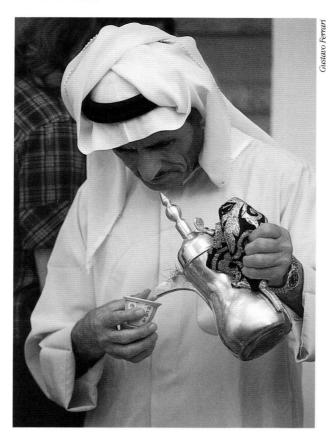

Gustavo Ferrari

Coffee is still a vital part of the ritual of hospitality.

Diwaniyas, gatherings for men only, often last until late.

Today, almost all of the bedu are completely settled in government housing areas. Prior to the invasion, a few still went into the desert whenever possible, but these days mines and military wreckage lie in the remoter areas. There is no longer the reliance on camels and their hair, and weaving was in danger of becoming a craft of the past. However, the government opened Al Sadu House next to the Bayt Al Badr on the Gulf Road in order to keep the craft alive. Young women can go to learn the craft from those who have known it for many years, and the unique traditional designs are kept alive in this way. Hospitality and loyalty were very important in the bedu code of conduct, and a prominent man would take care to have his coffee pot ready for surprise visitors. He would make the coffee himself, flavouring it with cardamom and serving it in thimble-like small cups.

Although the bedu are settled now it would seem that they retain their sense of austerity and that their houses are far less decorated than those of their town-dwelling counterparts. Some areas are predominantly bedu and the tribes played a large part in the National Assembly elections in 1992.

Family life today

There can be little doubt that life for the average family has changed considerably since the early years of the century. The family is still a powerful institution and the young people of today have not lost respect for their elders. The father is still the head of the family, the mother is still the lynch-pin.

Nevertheless, education and wealth have made some differences in areas such as segregation of the sexes. Marriages are more likely to occur between non-cousins, and the age of marrying is likely to be much older than it was in the past — but then the average life expectancy is longer too.

Weddings are major social occasions, calling for a display of finery not only on the part of bride and groom but also the guests. Diwaniyahs (male gatherings) remain the major point of social interchange for the men. Here anything from fishing to politics may be discussed; tea and coffee will be drunk, and men will linger until late at night. Meanwhile the women engage in tea parties and special dinners of their own.

Everyone is proud of their family name, whether it be the name of a mighty tribe or of a sub-division of a well-known family, or of an Utub family. Whatever else may change in Kuwait, that one point of loyalty is likely to remain constant.

The family is the central unit of Kuwaiti society. Children are seen as a gift from God, and hope for the future.

Traditional dancing is still performed on festive occasions.

Gustavo Ferrari

Islam

Kuwait is an Islamic country, and Islam is enshrined within the Kuwaiti Constitution. For the outsider there are many things to learn, and it is important that the religion is treated with absolute respect. There are five calls to prayer each day, the first coming at sunrise.

Islam stresses charity, and Kuwait gives a great deal to help others, even currently when the country needs every dinar it has for its own rebuilding programmes. Wealthy individuals are known to give the whole of their monthly salary to charity. Pilgrimage to Mecca is important, and Muslims are supposed to try to make the trip at least once in their lifetime.

Islam has an effect on the life of expatriates in Kuwait in as much as alcohol is forbidden and bacon and pork products are not available.

During Ramadan, the holy month of fasting, the whole pivot of the Kuwait day alters. Everything happens at night. It is forbidden to eat, drink, or smoke from dawn to dusk during this month, and people may well be fined or imprisoned if they violate these rules in public places. The month becomes a time for family get-togethers, with Eid Al Fitr, the holiday which marks the end of Ramadan, being a time of great festivity and celebration.

The ornately decorated door of the Kuwait Finance House.

Islam forms the basis of Kuwaiti society and beliefs.

THE GULF WAR

The present and 13th Emir of Kuwait, HH Sheikh Jaber Al Ahmad Al Jaber Al Sabah, came to the throne in the final hours of 1977. He took over a state which had developed enormously in his own lifetime, at a point in time when the rest of the world was heading for an economic slump.

In 1980, the northern Gulf was to lose a great deal of its own prosperity as the war between Iran and Iraq commenced. It ran for eight years in skirmishes reminiscent of the trench warfare of World War I. The conflict badly affected the economy of the region. Trade with Baghdad and Teheran ceased to a large extent, and new fears of being swallowed up by Khomeini's Iran gripped the region. Arab Iraq was seen as an ally and friend, and many of the small but wealthy states in the region gave financial and moral support to Iraq. Its leaders made the claim that they were protecting their smaller Arab brethren from the fundamentalist monster.

Kuwait, sharing its northern borders with Iraq, was perhaps one of the most adversely affected states. A campaign of terror began in the early 1980s with the bombing of the American Embassy, and the hijacking of a Kuwait Airways plane. The following years saw an assassination attempt against HH the Emir, and two bomb explosions in sea-front cafés which killed many people, young and old alike. A second hijacking, of a Kuwaiti 747, Al Jaberiyah, was to last for many days. Iranian missiles occasionally landed haphazardly in the desert and near the oilfields.

Yet these problems now seem insignificant compared with what was to come. It began as a tussle over oil outputs. Iraq accused Kuwait and the UAE of deliberately over-producing in order to

The Gulf War brought terrible devastation to Kuwait.

damage the economy of Iraq. The statement was met with incredulity in both countries, but then, most people were used to the sometimes bizarre rhetoric of Saddam Hussein. Even when he escalated the tension by moving his troops to the border, nobody thought that he would really invade. After all, had not Kuwait given Iraq billions in war loans? Had it not allowed Iraq to move its military aquisitions up through its territory? Had Kuwait not always been an ally? And had not Kuwait already suffered through its support of Iraq? Were they not brothers? And only months before, the Emir had been present at a conference in Baghdad. It was generally thought that Saddam wanted concessions, particularly the cancelling of those war loans, and that on meeting recalcitrance from the Kuwait Government, was attempting a little coercion.

Everybody was convinced that the meeting in Jeddah on 1st August, 1990 would solve everything. *Arab Times* went to press only hours before the invasion with the headline, "Jeddah talks end... more needed". *Kuwait Times* matched it with "Kuwait hopes for more talks".

Many Iraqi soldiers died for their leader's stubbornness.

The sound of gunfire

That was all shattered in the early hours of 2nd August, 1990. While the rest of the world slept, Kuwait awakened to the sound of gunfire. In the West, and elsewhere in the world, only a sketchy picture could be formed of what was actually happening inside Kuwait. Saddam's forces had apparently swept over the border and taken the country with no opposition.

However, this was not the truth. Although the military had been placed on red alert, the orders to fight were slow in coming, partly because the government was afraid that any sign of immediate resistance would allow the Iraqis to claim that it was Kuwaiti soldiers who started the fighting.

Resistance was mobilised. There was heavy fighting for control over the Jiwan army camp to the north of the city, and the 35th Brigade, led by Colonel Salem Masoud and supported by sections of the tank corps, mounted heavy resistance in the Muttla Ridge area. Fighting continued from the early hours of the morning until late afternoon. Yet a tiny fighting force can never be a match for one of the largest armies in the world. The accounts by the men who fought that day tell of continual

The Iraqis enforced the use of different licence plates for cars — here they lie in a discarded heap after liberation.

treachery by the Iraqi forces. White flags were hoisted, and when the Kuwaiti forces moved forwards to accept their surrender the flag would come down and they would be fired upon. Members of the 35th Brigade, now known as the Martyrs' Brigade, tell of seeing a line of what appeared to be friendly tanks approaching, only to realise at the last moment that they were hostile.

Ironically, if the Kuwaitis were confused, the Iraqi soldiers themselves were more so. Some berated the Kuwaitis for firing on them. Some stopped civilians and asked where they were, to be surprised at the answer. Some thought that they were attacking Israel, and still others thought they were on GCC manoeuvres.

Within 24 hours any organised military response to the invasion from Kuwait was over. Those soldiers who managed to escape the camps, or who moved quickly away from their homes were

to form the core of the Resistance movement. Those that did not, spent the whole of the seven-month period from Occupation to Liberation as "guests of Saddam Hussein" in Iraq, a euphemism for the most brutal and harsh captiviy.

The Resistance consisted of a number of cells under the nominal command of Interior Minister Sheikh Salem Al Sabah. Each cell was virtually autonomous, often with a military man at the head. Many of these cell commanders were members of the Al Sabah family, despite the claims in the media of the West that they had all fled.

In fact it was only the Government that fled. Had the forces managed to capture the Emir there would have been no legitimate government to restore, and perhaps nothing to fight for. By escaping, and only in the nick of time, the Kuwait Government robbed them of that opportunity. It is clear that this was a key part of Saddam's plan, as for 24 hours he had nothing to say, other than to issue the chilling threat that if the West intervened, he would turn Kuwait into a graveyard. And the world, remembering what he had done to Halabja with his chemical weapons, feared that he would use them again.

It is now clear that Saddam's forces made two initial mistakes. The first was that they did not capture the Emir. The second was that they under-estimated the amount of resistance they would meet. There is considerable speculation that he intended to sweep down the eastern coast of Arabia before anyone could stop him. Saddam's next mistake was, once the world had responded, not pulling back to the north of Jahra. Had he done so, it is unlikely that such an enormous military response would have been agreed upon, and he would probably have got away with annexing the islands of Bubiyan and Warba, and the Rumailah oilfields he wanted so much.

Many died in the fighting that day, including Sheikh Fahad Al Ahmed, younger brother of the Emir, who was gunned down at the palace.

The troops dig in

Saddam said that he would start to withdraw his forces, moving tanks towards the north in an effort to convince the spy satellites that he was doing so. It was just captured Kuwaiti tanks he was moving, and those who are used to his rhetoric believe that when he said he was pulling his troops out of Kuwait he meant it, only not towards home, but towards Saudi and the lower Gulf.

The world was swift in mobilising a response; they froze Iraqi assets, and did the same to Kuwaiti ones in order to protect them. They issued resolutions calling for sanctions. Inside Kuwait people were in a state of shock. Saddam claimed that his forces had been invited into Kuwait by revolutionaries. The world saw through this immediately. He had hoped to capitalise on the activities of the Opposition, which prior to the invasion had been vociferous and anti-government. He tried in vain to find an Opposition figure who would agree to form a puppet government, and had to face the fact that although the Oppostion had indeed criticised Government policy, that did not mean that it was anti-Kuwait. How could he understand that Kuwait allowed freedom of speech

Iraqi tanks dug in for battle expecting the trench warfare of the Iran-Iraq War.

and that the Opposition had the right to speak out? After all, anyone speaking out against his own regime would have been tortured, probably forced to witness the torture of his family, and then shot.

The men who were chosen to form the provisional government were lightweights and puppets, and mostly Iraqis. They commanded no loyalty whatsoever, and after a time Saddam simply dispensed with them, appointing his cousin, Ali Hassan Al Majid, one of the most feared men in Iraq, as governor.

The hostages

The world's eyes were on the hostages, those expatriates who, because their home governments were taking a hard line against Saddam, were rounded up and used as human shields. And while he committed atrocities in Kuwait he could always release a few hostages here and there to make the anti-war lobbies in the West believe that it was possible to negotiate with him. The hostages and their families suffered dreadfully. Some of that suffering was physical, much of it was psychological. For many the trauma continues.

And for the Kuwaitis the world became an ugly place. Many fled from the country, others stayed. Most people tried to get on with their lives as best they could, and to help those who needed help. Many joined the Resistance.

Right and below: Kuwait's suqs were emptied of all produce and goods. Those who tried to shop for essentials ran the risk of being rounded up by the Iraqis.

Kuwait's Resistance

The Resistance maintained a number of activities which were to be vital in the efforts to liberate the country. It had a number of satellite phones which were used to brief those outside about what was happening — troop movements and so on. They also allowed contact between those trapped inside and their loved ones abroad, a vital morale booster at a time of need. They distributed cash to those who needed it, and also paid the ransoms demanded by the Iraqi troops for Kuwaiti men, women and children.

There were also some hot-heads who would try to shoot anything or anybody connected with the Iraqis in any way, and their activities and their tendency to brag about it on television when they arrived outside the country led to increasingly severe reprisals. These people do not seem to have been closely associated with the real Resistance.

For some, being involved with the Resistance involved driving a garbage truck as a cover — underneath the rotting rubbish would be a cache of weapons. The driver would bank on the guards at check-points being put off by the stench. Others transported Resistance newsletters around the city. This was another vital morale booster, to keep communications up. Still others manned vital services, worked in bakeries, delivering bread to the homes of those who could not travel, and to the foreigners in hiding. Men, women, girls and boys worked to keep Kuwait going, to keep Kuwait alive.

On another level there were those who saw not the return of Kuwait and its legitimate government, but momentary advantage. Almost every nationality had its looters and thieves. Brother stole from brother, colleague from colleague, and those who left the country, or who had been away at the time of the invasion were unlikely to have anything left when they returned. It may well have been the Iraqis who took it, but it might equally have been anyone else.

The problem was compounded by the influx of scores of Iraqi peasants and Palestinians whose only intention was to take as much as they could. Eye witnesses who were passing out through the Jordan border report hundreds of cars going the other way, heading for the rich pickings in Kuwait. Many Palestinians who had lived in Kuwait all their lives fought in the Resistance, and were as strongly in support of their home as the Kuwaitis. There were also those who collaborated.

Teams from across the world battled to put out the fires.

Margaret Thatcher and HH the Emir with the children of the missing.

Hossam Al Sayafe: arrested in 1990, he has not returned.

Atrocity upon atrocity

The reprisals and tortures carried out by the Iraqis were terrible. Torture on a previously unimaginable scale became the norm, as did summary executions. No Kuwaiti was safe, even in his home. Young men were taken, tortured, returned home and shot in front of their familes, who were then forbidden to collect the bodies from the street. Women, girls, men, boys, and even young children were raped. Children were executed for singing the national anthem, or hanged for no good reason. The entire population was brutalised.

The Iraqis set up a number of torture and detention centres. Those who survived are left physically, emotionally and mentally scarred. Those who did not, were often brought to the Kuwait morgue for burial. There a group of Kuwaiti doctors, including Dr Abdulla Al Hammadi, photographed them and detailed their injuries, keeping their documentation for the future, in the hope that those responsible could be brought to trial. Dr Hammadi published his evidence, together with photographs, in a book which was not allowed on general release — it was simply too awful to bear.

He gives the names of the Iraqi soldiers and officers responsible for removing items from the hospitals, and has documentary evidence for each charge, as he and his colleagues pursuaded them to sign receipts and other papers. All the while, he and his colleagues were risking their lives to try to make sure that the truth would one day be told. Dr Hammadi was not only there when the babies were removed from the incubators, but he buried them himself. In his book he even lists their names and those of their parents. There were claims in the West that this incident never happened, but his book shows that these babies were people, members of families, and that their deaths were a cause for grief, not propaganda.

The missing

Atrocities were committed as a matter of course, but the worst of these continue to this day. Nearly a thousand Kuwaitis, who were arrested and reported as being taken to Iraq, are still missing. Their families are in agony as they wait. Now, more than two years later, some are beginning to despair.

Those missing include men, women and even children. Hossam Al Sayafe ran a thriving marine business in Salmiyah. He was arrested in October

Towering flames lit the sky above blazing oil wells.

A crew struggles to stop a gushing well.

or November 1990, and has not returned. He was one of the kindest men alive and his friends loved him dearly. If ever he saw anyone with a problem, no matter what their nationality, he would do his utmost to help them. He was a brave, strong, vibrant and warm person who loved his parents, and who was proud of being a Kuwaiti.

Nawaf Al Wazzan was a student who was studying in America. When he heard of the invasion he managed to get back inside the country to be with his family. He too, is missing, as are so many others like him whose only crime was to love their country. The POWs (as they are called in Kuwait, though most were civilians, kidnapped for no valid reason), are people, with rights and needs, and for the most part they are being ignored as the western world turns its attention to something more newsworthy. The scale of suffering during the Occupation was tremendous, and still continues to this day. If these people are alive they must be returned. If not then that fact must be established, setting their families free from useless waiting and cruel hope, and allowing them to grieve properly.

The moment after the fire has been put out but before the well is under control.

Desert Storm

The torture and rapes, the murders and brutalities make one almost despair of humanity. That the world did in fact unite behind Kuwait and that it formed a coalition force to rescue the Kuwaiti people, does a great deal to restore a little faith. Thirty-five countries formed the force which finally liberated Kuwait on 26th February, 1991. For the most part, Kuwait's Arab allies were staunchly supportive. Saudi Arabia allowed its lands to be used as a springboard for the war to liberate Kuwait, and Egypt and Syria were both strong and vociferous in their condemnation of Iraq and support for the UN resolutions. Other Gulf states provided havens for those displaced by the invasion.

The allies did everything possible to get unanimous world consent for their actions, and continued negotiating, or rather, attempting to negotiate with the intractable Saddam, almost until the last moment. Finally a deadline of 15th January, 1991 was named for Saddam to withdraw, or to start his withdrawal from Kuwait. This came and went, and in the small hours of January 16th the air war began.

Flames mirrored in lakes of oil: Saddam brought a new concept of 'environmental terrorism' to a horrified world.

Trenches were prepared along Kuwait's coastline.

Pilots of many nationalities, but predominantly American, British, French, Kuwaiti and Saudi Arabian flew almost continual missions throughout this phase of the offensive. Here was a high-tech war, with smart bombs and cruise missiles that made the enemy's response look puny and inadequate.

Everyone dreaded the ground war. Saddam's troops had shown themselves to be masters of trench warfare, and it was feared that the push to liberate Kuwait could take months. Saddam himself threatened the world with "the mother of all battles," before being forced to accept the mother of all defeats.

It is clear that Saddam expected the threat to come from the sea. In fact the infantries of the coalition were speeding to the north to cut off Kuwait from Iraq. The whole of the ground offensive took only a few days, with reports that the Allied soldiers were being hampered not by resistance from the enemy, but by the fact that they were surrendering in droves.

For those inside Kuwait there was tremendous joy and elation, then dismay as the damage was surveyed. In an attempt to block the allies, and also probably to destroy Kuwait if he could not keep it, Saddam had ordered the firing of the oil wells, and a slick of oil was deliberately released into the Gulf by his men. They also damaged desalination and electricity plants. The liberators found a Kuwait with no food, no communications, no electricity, and no water. The task of rebuilding was to be an immense one. Experts estimated that it would take more than five years to cap all the oil well fires. They said that the fragile ecosystem of the Gulf would be damaged forever. Some days dawn never came as the burning wells belched black smoke high into the sky. Soot from the fires was found as far away as on the snows of the mountains of Afghanistan.

The burning wells belched black smoke high into the sky.

Gustavo Ferrari

A NEW
BEGINNING

During the Iraqi Occupation of Kuwait, Saddam Hussein had painstakingly kept the eyes of the world away from what he called the 19th province of Iraq, Kazima. Inevitably therefore, the liberators were appalled by the damage they found, much of it senseless and spiteful. It was known from Resistance reports and other sources, that great damage had been done to Kuwait's infrastructure, but even so, the world was unprepared for the extent of plunder that was found. Everything that could be removed had been taken. The food lorries which trundled in from Saudi Arabia could not travel fast enough for Kuwait's inhabitants.

The problems of re-establishing some semblance of normal life were compounded by the fact that there were still Iraqi soldiers and collaborators in hiding. Whilst the military worked to flush them out, it also had to prevent the young hot-heads, who had perhaps been on the fringes of the Resistance, but most probably had spent the Occupation outside Kuwait and had now returned, from taking the law into their own hands, and from rounding up people by national grouping regardless of whether they had supported or fought against the Occupation and regardless of whether or not they had collaborated or had helped Kuwaitis to survive.

Martial Law was declared, headed by the Crown Prince of Kuwait, Sheikh Saad Al Abdullah Al Sabah, and work started immediately on restoring the vital services of the country and also on rounding up as many of the weapons as possible which were still lying around. It is a measure of the success of the restoration of government and control that the initial period of military rule was not extended.

Kuwait's youth stride towards a new, bright future.

Communications with the outside world were available only through satellite phones, again due to damage done by the retreating Iraqis. AT&T, the famous US phone company, made a link available free to Kuwaitis and the airwaves were jammed with those who had stayed and survived calling their loved ones and friends all round the world to tell them that they were safe, but that Kuwait was not yet a good or safe place to come home to.

At noon, if the wind was blowing towards the city, the sky would be completely black, the sun blocked out totally by the smoke from the blazing oil wells. About 727 wells had been fired in the last days and final hours of the Occupation. This was an oilfield calamity on a scale that had never been seen before and Red Adair, the famed Texan firefighter, who had held a virtual monopoly in capping oilfield fires over a 50-year period prepared to move in. However, it was a job that was too big for one crew alone. Two other crews from the US and one from Canada, joined him in the initial stages of the battle to put out the oil fires.

Subsequently, would-be firefighters of 28 different nationalities flooded into the country, and some immensely resourceful methods were used. The Hungarian team used two jet engines, mounted on an old tank body, to blow out the flames. The Kuwaiti firefighting team included Sarah Akbar, who had been instrumental in saving the records of the oil company. These records provided detailed information about each well, and were to prove vital in the multi-national effort to extinguish the fires.

The task of putting the flames out was hampered by the amount of smoke being belched into the sky. Much of the time the teams couldn't even see as they tried to drive from well to well and there were fatalities when jeeps left the road and skidded into the mine fields. There were also booby traps left by the Iraqis to contend with. Nevertheless, well by well, flame by flame, the fires were extinguished. The last well was capped in November 1991, just eight months after western scientists had predicted that it would take five to ten years to extinguish them all.

Fires were extinguished in an astoundingly short time.

Mine clearance was another vitally important aspect of the pre-rebuilding work. The beaches had to be swept, and the buildings of the city, particularly those which had been occupied by the Iraqis, were booby-trapped. The post-liberation death toll amongst civilians killed in accidents involving mines or other explosive ordnance was frighteningly high, and more than two years after the invasion, mines and bombs are still being found in Kuwait.

Every step the liberators took had to be taken with care; Kuwaiti soldiers manning road blocks were fired upon on more than one occasion and the last Iraqis were still being rounded up a year after the Kuwaiti flag had been hoisted in the flag square again. At the same time there was a security nightmare as those who had been in Iraq returned. The reunion with their families was often delayed as security forces tried to establish whether they were genuine returnees or Iraqi infiltrators.

Rebuilding the infrastructure

Before the invasion, there were six major power-generating plants in Kuwait, as well as some experimental sites. Kuwait's government-in-exile returned to find that all installations had been seriously damaged and dismantled by the retreating invaders. However, power was restored and work continues on repairing the whole network.

As Kuwait is a country with no rivers or water resources other than a few subterranean wells of varying potable quality, the country's desalination plants were of vital importance to the country's existence and development as an industrial nation. These desalination plants were systematically dismantled, and the cost of repairing the damage to pipeline networks, water wells and distribution and control centres is about 56 million Kuwaiti dinars.

Again, the hospitals, once amongst the best-equipped in the world, were plundered of almost every piece of equipment and item of medicine. Although some of the equipment has been returned to Kuwait, most of what has come back is in an unusable condition or has been irrevocably damaged. Education also suffered, with all laboratory equipment at Kuwait University and Kuwait Institute for Scientific Research being taken to Iraq. Some schools were used as bases by the Iraqis, some as torture centres. The work of cleaning these up has been difficult and distressing. All Kuwait's children missed out on their academic programme, but the schools are up and running

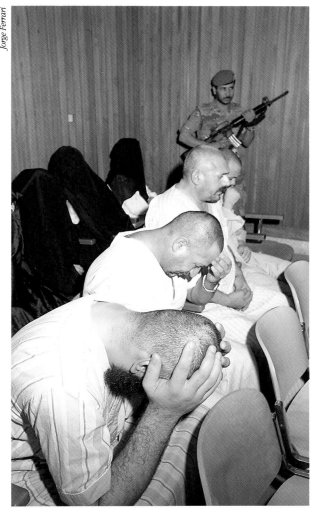

Collaborators were rounded up for trial.

Power-generating plants were seriously damaged.

Oil installations in Kuwait were among the most advanced in the world; after damage by the Iraqis, rebuilding is under way.

again, and teachers are striving to make up as much lost time as possible, recognising that Kuwait's future lies with its children.

Kuwait's transportation network was also badly hit. Terminal One at Kuwait Airport (the old terminal) was completely destroyed, the runway and main terminal building were badly damaged, and Iraq took many of Kuwait's aircraft for itself. Again, those returned were in an appalling state. The losses suffered by Kuwait Airways alone are estimated at 382 million Kuwaiti dinars, including the cost of 15 aeroplanes, nine engines, spare parts, equipment and tools.

The roads were damaged, and major projects halted. Every bus was taken to Iraq. The ports were excessively vandalised, with damage estimated in excess of 100 million Kuwaiti dinars, plus 50 million dinars which is required to replace the equipment and clear mines. The communications network was brought to a total standstill by the Iraqis as they retreated. This area received the necessary priority in rebuilding, but even so it took months before it was possible to place an overseas call.

Prior to the invasion, Kuwait had spent a considerable sum on the 'greening of Kuwait'. The invaders pulled trees out of the ground in places, but in many landscaped areas it was simply neglect and lack of water which killed the plants. These are

now being replaced. Agriculture of a limited nature was carried out in various areas of Kuwait, notably Jahra to the north of Kuwait, and Wafra, close to the southern border with Saudi Arabia. Tomatoes, melons, cucumbers, onions, courgettes and marrows, of a good standard, were all supplied to the local market. Mine-clearance has been necessary in the Wafra area, but HH the Emir has announced even more ambitious measures to encourage agriculture in Kuwait. 700,000 Kuwaiti dinars has been allocated to promote the growing of wheat, and in order to encourage citizens to take advantage of the project, the government will buy all wheat grown for double its price on world markets.

Kuwait's heritage was also severely threatened. The museums were totally gutted, old houses were irrevocably damaged and the beautiful old boom, or large dhow, which stood in the courtyard of the museums complex was burnt to the ground. The National Museum held artefacts found on Failika, and items of importance to the self-awareness of the Kuwaiti people. One of Kuwait's most important and valuable collections belonged to

Right: Local produce had been marketed successfully.
Below: The refurbishment of Kuwait's ports have enabled them to resume their role in the service and support of the country's economy.

The flag square on the Kuwait sea front is the focus of national celebrations to mark the anniversary of independence — and of the liberation.

Sheikh Nasser Sabah Al Ahmad Al Sabah and his wife, Sheikha Hussa Sabah Al Salem Al Sabah. They had painstakingly collected beautiful and unique examples of Islamic art in all its variety, from huge old doors, to priceless rugs and rare books, to pottery, china and jewellery. All this was once on show to the public in a special building in the museums complex. Everything was taken by the Iraqis.

"They were very organised," says Sheikha Hussa. "They knew what they had come for and everything they took was itemised and inventoried." Even so, some rare pieces including old books were damaged by the journey to Iraq.

Although the bulk of the treasures have been returned, a lot will need restoration, and some of the most valuable, in particular some priceless emeralds, are still missing. Sheikha Hussa is now looking for a new site to house the collection, feeling that the old building should be kept in its dreadful condition as a reminder of what happened.

Private sector companies had to resume trading in appallingly difficult conditions, but gradually confidence was restored and the business economy began to pick up. The Kuwait stock market resumed its operations in late 1992, to see brisk, if cautious trading.

Kuwait's stock market resumed trading in late 1992.

Gustavo Ferrari

The well-designed Ministries Complex houses five ministries.

Nobody knows why the Iraqis damaged the main suq.

A return to the old life

Immediately after the Kuwaitis were able to return to their homeland the country became a shopkeeper's paradise, as everyone sought to replace the essential items which had been stolen, lost or damaged during the Occupation period. The car dealers and furniture salesrooms had a boom period, but prices and the cost of living rose drastically as Kuwait's manufacturing capacity was eliminated and everything, from cakes to cutlery, needed to be imported from outside.

The pictures of jubilant Kuwaitis celebrating the liberation of their country were beamed across the world. But within days the euphoria died. Life was harsh; in some ways things were harder than during the Occupation. People were missing, people were dead. Now that the pressure was off, the pains of the months of terror surfaced as anxieties, resentments and griefs.

It is clear that Kuwait can never be exactly the same again. Those trapped outside the country during the Occupation had one thought with which they encouraged themselves daily; Kuwait would be restored and be better than before. Yet when they returned they found life difficult and traumatic.

On the whole, people are now more hard-working, more serious, and many are more religious. Terrible scars lurk under the surface of Kuwaiti society. For many, coping with the fact that their loved ones are still being held by Iraq is a painful experience. The Government has been supportive and has provided care and assistance for the families of those still held, as well as trying to mobilise support on an international level.

Many of those who have returned from Iraq, or who were released from detention, have the physical scars of torture to remind them of their ordeal. Some scars go deeper still. The Government established the Al Riqqa Clinic for Post-Traumatic Stress Disorders, staffed by two European specialists, as well as Kuwaiti physicians, psychologists and psychiatrists. Part of the difficulty, according to Dr Bothayna, a child psychologist based at the clinic, is getting people to accept that they have a problem which is a normal result of what has happened, and that seeking treatment is no shame. The clinic has embarked on a programme in Kuwait's schools, training families and teachers to recognise symptoms, and encouraging them to seek the professional help that the clinic provides. The clinic treats everyone, regardless of nationality.

The joy and euphoria of liberation cannot overcome the sadness for the dead, the missing and the destruction.

Expatriate Kuwait

Many of Kuwait's inhabitants are expatriates, of a wide variety of different nationalities. Kuwait has a small population, with a high proportion of children too young to work. In past years therefore, Kuwait had to rely on foreigners to keep vital services running.

Prior to the invasion it was already recognised that this was a dangerous social trend, as Kuwaitis were outnumbered by expatriates. There was increasing talk of training Kuwait's students to meet future manpower requirements, and also of the Kuwaitisation of all possible jobs.

Kuwait is now rationalising its demographic structure. It aims to keep the population at around 1.2 million persons, with a much lower percentage of expatriates. More and more young Kuwaitis are now entering the labour force, and it is held to be vital that they can find work.

Nevertheless, expatriates are treated well in Kuwait, pay no income tax, and are protected by the excellent and comprehensive Kuwait Labour Law. Many of the expatriates currently working in Kuwait have been in the country for over 20 years and regard it as their home.

A raft race gets underway.

Long-term effects of the oil pollution are not yet known.

Democracy

HH the Emir, Sheikh Jaber Al Ahmad Al Jaber Al Sabah promised the Kuwaiti people that their right to hold free elections to the National Assembly would be restored. In October 1992, those eligible to vote in Kuwait went to the polls and elected 50 deputies, two from each of 25 constituencies. A new government was formed, featuring a higher number of elected members than ever in the past. A new era of co-operation between the legislative and executive powers began, with a series of resolutions, to amend the Constitution, to allow women, and those without full nationality rights, the right to vote, and to reduce the age requirement for voters to 18 years. The so-called 'August 2nd

file' was also opened, in an attempt, not to cast blame, but to recognise the reasons behind the invasion. Kuwait's political life is already healthier, and Opposition and pro-Government Kuwaitis alike are optimistic about Kuwait's future.

However, Kuwait had to borrow internationally in order to finance the massive rebuilding programme, and though oil reserves have not been significantly damaged, production is not yet at capacity. Again, the fact that over 700 oil wells were burning over a 258-day period has resulted in a great deal of pollution. An increase in bronchial and chest infections has been reported, along with a rise in skin and other allergies. It is not yet clear exactly how bad the damage has been, and whether or not there will be long-term effects on the region and its people.

LEISURE IN KUWAIT

Before the invasion, leisure time could be packed with activity or approached at a more relaxed pace. There was plenty to do, and many social gatherings of both a formal and casual nature were held.

Inevitably, leisure facilities and, to some extent even the urge to socialise, suffered because of the Occupation. Celebrations to mark the first anniversary of liberation were cancelled by His Highness, the Emir, as a mark of respect for those still held in Iraq and their families.

The waterfront project stretched from Kuwait Towers to Salmiyah and featured beaches, beach-side cafés, children's playgrounds, swimming pools and a man-made island. Although it was only completed a short time before the invasion, it was badly damaged, partly through vandalism, partly through spite. Happily, this has now been restored, and people can again walk along the promenades in the cool evening hours. However, though a massive sum has been spent on mine clearance, there are still warnings about the inadvisability of walking on the beaches, mainly because it is still possible that mines may be washed ashore. A shallow-water clearance project has begun, and many waterfront establishments, like the SAS Hotel, are placing nets across the entries to their beaches to ensure that no mine comes ashore. The problem is likely to diminish as time passes, and the public is well primed with warnings to call the Ministry of Defence if anything resembling a weapon or mine is sighted.

Sadly, another old tradition has had to be abandoned, for the time-being at least. It was previously the custom to travel into the desert in the early, cooler months of the year, and to set up camp there. Sometimes entire families would sleep

Sailing is a popular sport in Kuwait.

in the desert instead of at home, and villages of tents would grow up in the more popular areas. However, 'primitive' is not necessarily a word which springs to mind in this respect! Some camps had hot and cold running water, and electricity provided by generators. In these more luxurious versions of Kuwaiti camping, there was likely to be the traditional camel hair tent, and also the more common canvas marquees, complete with television and stereo. No doubt, if this custom were still possible today, we would see some enterprising camper erecting a satellite dish! Sadly, the presence of mines and unexploded ordnance renders such camps foolhardy and unpractical today, but those lucky enough to attend them in the past will never forget the experience.

A vast amount of explosive ordnance was left behind.

Kuwait's people in general come either from desert or seafaring stock. Not surprisingly therefore, Kuwait's people spend a great deal of time on, in or by the sea; and that makes sense in the summer when only the cooling sea breeze brings comfort from the heat.

Every watersport yet devised by man has been, is, or will be practised again in Kuwait. One of the most popular new sports prior to the invasion was powerboat racing. Although it is only now becoming possible to plan a major Kuwait race again, Kuwait's racers have travelled to Dubai and further afield to race. Khalifa Al Qatami and Sheikh Basil Salem Al Sabah both competed in American events, and in 1991, only months after he was released from an Iraqi prison, Ahmed Al Ansari won the World 6-litre Championship in Norway.

For those who like their boating to be a little less frenetic there are yacht clubs and slipways, and prior to the invasion, an impressive fleet of motor yachts and fishing boats was moored in Kuwait's waters. Many of these boats were deliberately sunk in the harbour, or taken to Iraq. They are being restored, renovated or replaced, and on any calm Thursday or Friday throughout the year Kuwait's boating enthusiasts can be seen out in force.

Windsurfing is also popular, particularly as the prevailing conditions most of the year are mild. Sail boat racing has also been hugely popular, but the Iran-Iraq war hit activities, forcing the clubs concerned to cancel the Kuwait-Bahrain race. Diving, parascending, water-skiing and jet ski racing remain popular.

As a country, Kuwait invests extensively in its sportsmen and government-funded clubs exist for almost every sport. The favourite sport in Kuwait remains football, but tennis, squash and basketball are also popular. In the early months of 1992 Kuwait hosted a squash tournament which brought some of the world's best players, including Jehangir Khan, to Kuwait.

Sports in Kuwait come under the umbrella of the Ministry of Social Affairs and Labour. The Olympic Association, headed by Sheikh Ahmed Fahad Al Ahmed, son of the martyred Sheikh Fahad Al Ahmed, provides many with the opportunity and funding to pursue their sporting careers and ambitions.

Motor rallies have also been highly popular in the past and the first rally in post-liberation Kuwait was held in January 1993, on a route specially prepared by the government in an area guaranteed to be free from mines.

Jet-skis have become a familiar sight in Kuwait Bay.

The Al Shayer boat races in Dubai.

A wind-surfing race at Messilah Beach.

Children enjoy participating in parades and celebrations.

Other sports, such as golf, archery, rugby and cricket all have venues in Kuwait, both for citizens and expatriates, and opportunities for competitive matches abound.

Swimming facilities can be found either at the Touristic Enterprises Company Swimming Pools Complex on the sea front, or at the various sea clubs. Hotel health clubs are very popular and all are well-equipped but only the SAS Hotel, the Regency Palace and the Messilah Beach health clubs have a beach.

A great deal of the social life of Kuwait takes place at the country's leading hotels — the Kuwait International, the Meridien, the Regency Palace, the SAS Hotel, the Sheraton and the Holiday Inn. Each of these hotels has a number of restaurants offering different specialities, and there are opportunities to sample French, Italian, Chinese, Japanese and even Iranian cuisine.

The Touristic Enterprises Company has a number of entertainment facilities, including the Green Island on the sea front. This is a man-made island featuring a lagoon and observation points, and forms the centrepiece of the waterfront project.

The Kuwait Towers, perhaps the most well-known symbol of the country in the post-invasion period, have been reconstructed and refurbished and the revolving roof-top restaurant and observation platforms are open.

The Towers feature observation decks and a restaurant.

Touristic Enterprises has also restored Entertainment City, a funfair complete with roller-coaster and other rides. The Iraqis dismantled most of what was there, but the City is up and running again.

Shopping is a national pastime, and almost every item under the sun can be found in Kuwait, with the obvious exception of those items banned. The Sultan Center in Salmiyah is probably the city's most popular supermarket, and a wide variety of food and other goods can be found there, ranging from items associated with local cuisine, to health conscious products flown in from Europe and America.

Meat, vegetables and dairy products are all of a high standard, and there is no need for the newcomer to Kuwait to have to look far for what he wants at a reasonable price.

Salmiyah and Kuwait City both have extensive modern shopping areas which sell every electrical item yet thought of by man, and high fashion and traditional clothing. Other shopping complexes, such as the Zahra Complex in Salmiyah, and the Salhiyah and Al Mutthana complexes in Kuwait City provide a shopping experience along American lines. And of course, Kuwait's old suqs still bustle with activity.

Everything suffered during the Occupation period, but the country has already gone a long way towards re-establishing the best of what was in Kuwait before.

Al Mutthana Complex, a modern shopping experience in the heart of Kuwait.

THE HOTEL INDUSTRY

After liberation, Kuwait was visited by an incoming tide of foreign businessmen and journalists. Most hotels had been occupied by the Iraqis, and almost all were damaged to some degree by the retreating armies, presumably to conceal information and destroy evidence.

The Sheraton was set alight; the ground and first floors of the Meridien Hotel were burnt out; and the front and upper floors of the Kuwait International Hotel — renamed the Safir International Kuwait — were fired upon. The Ramada Hotel, which had once been a cruise liner and which overlooked the sea next to the port, was also completely burnt down. The beach-front hotels, the Regency Palace and the SAS Kuwait Hotel were amongst the most badly damaged.

Some hotels were up and running within months, while others took longer to reconstruct. The Safir International Kuwait Hotel's greenery and gardens have been painstakingly brought back to life by the dedication and hard work of the gardening team and the grounds are blooming once again with a multitude of flowers from the hotel's own greenhouse.

The SAS Kuwait Hotel was damaged only two hours or so before the end of the war, when the Iraqis set it on fire as they withdrew. They planted incendiary devices and bombs, and hurled grenades into the rooms. The hotel has now been rebuilt and, as a positive response to the challenge, refurbished in a massive upgrading of facilities. Thankfully, its popular restaurant, the Al Boom, was virtually undamaged by the invaders. A replica of one of the largest types of traditional sailing craft used in Kuwait, the Al Boom continues to look out over the now peaceful seas.

Ironically, Kuwait's hotels have seen more business since the liberation, and are now thriving again.

With life returning to normal, Kuwait's beaches are once again attracting residents and tourists.

Guestrooms are well-appointed and equipped with modern amenities.

The hotel's banqueting facilities are spacious and tastefully decorated.

The Holiday Inn Crowne Plaza, Kuwait, with its imposing glass structure, offers a high standard of service and quality.

HOLIDAY INN CROWNE PLAZA KUWAIT

The imposing glass structure of the Holiday Inn Crowne Plaza, Kuwait stands just three kilometres away from Kuwait International Airport. Located approximately 11 kilometres from the city centre, five kilometres from both the Shuwaikh and Subhan industrial areas and another five kilometres from the International Exhibition Grounds, it is also within easy access of the Ahmadi oil refineries and the Jahra and Doha centres, linked by an extensive motorway system.

The hotel offers a high level of service and quality. All the 389 guestrooms — standard and deluxe suites and a Royal Suite — are fully air-conditioned with individual temperature controls. Each room is also equipped with a mini fridge, colour TV with in-house movies and satellite channels, radio and an automatic wake-up call. The telephone system offers an automatic voice-mail feature.

A variety of gift shops and a bank are located in the lobby, while the gents and ladies hairdressers are on the first floor. The Al Ahmadi Restaurant, also in the lobby, offers a view of the swimming pool, and serves an international buffet for breakfast, lunch and dinner as well as an à la carte menu. A children's menu is also available. The restaurant features special theme nights throughout the week when it hosts a gourmet trip around the world.

The Al Andalus Seafood Restaurant is open for dinner only every evening except Fridays, where guests can enjoy a selection of fresh seafood cooked to their liking. The newly opened Sakura Restaurant offers traditional Japanese cuisine in authentic surroundings — teppanyaki, shabu-shabu, sushi and sashimi, all served by kimono-clad waitresses.

For a light snack, refreshments or ice-cream, the Vienna Café is open from 10am to 11pm in the evening.

The Gardens, overlooking the atrium and the lobby serve light snacks, refreshments, tea and coffee, and hubbly-bubbly.

During the season, the Shahrazad Barbeque is held around the swimming pool every Wednesday night.

The Holiday Inn Crowne Plaza, Kuwait also provides comprehensive banqueting and conference facilities, with a Grand Ballroom capable of accommodating up to 400 people.

For sports lovers, the Apollo Fitness Centre has the latest in fitness equipment; five squash courts, two floodlit tennis courts, an outdoor temperature-controlled swimming pool, a four-lane bowling alley and a choice of activities such as Taekwando, Judo etc.

The Holiday Inn Crowne Plaza, Kuwait was originally opened in May 1982 and is owned by the Al Houda Hotels and Tourism Company.

The spacious lobby of the hotel displays a bank and a variety of gift shops which are very popular with guests and visitors.

SAFIR INTERNATIONAL KUWAIT

The Safir International Kuwait, formerly the Kuwait International Hotel, is centrally located and overlooks the Arabian Gulf. Swaying palms line the driveway, leading from an artistically designed rock garden near the main road to the main entrance where guests step through another rock garden and rows of flowers with illuminated domes overhead.

Refurbished and well-equipped rooms offer 16 TV and cable channels for indoor entertainment. In addition, the hotel has 65 telephone lines for the benefit of the business traveller. The conversion of some guestrooms into mini apartments with a kitchenette has proved popular.

To cope with the increasing amount of business, plans to extend the existing fully-equipped Business Centre include addition of a spacious sitting area, a conference table for six, and several personal computers for guests to work on individually. The Centre also procures business visas for guests free of charge.

This five-star hotel offers a busy and lively atmosphere to its upmarket clientele. The stream of promotions at La Patisserie is a constant attraction and its early morning Breakfast Ride from 7am is popular even with non-residents. Specialities include a variety of fresh breads and juices, croissants, daily newspapers, CNN/BBC.

The Failaka Restaurant, situated on the 19th floor is manned by a team of French chefs and Restaurant Manager. A window table, for which bookings should be made in advance, offers a view of the symbolic Kuwait Towers.

Above left: Lush greenery and colourful flowers greet the visitor as he approaches the sweeping driveway of the Safir International Kuwait.

Below: The Executive Lounge offers various facilities to Executive Floor guests.

The cool, serene interior of the Businessman's Suite on the Japanese Floor is perfect for unwinding after a hard day.

La Palma has a more casual ambience with its culinary trips offering a series of theme nights during the week. It will also be the venue for a weekly food and beverage promotion, The Car Park, providing an appetising selection of food.

The Executive Lounge on the Executive Floor, open from 7am to 11pm daily, offers complimentary continental breakfast, fruits, snacks and soft drinks.

The hotel's Japanese Floor features Teppanyaki rooms artfully designed and modelled to suit the Japanese lifestyle. The Japanese Restaurant offers a soothing, oriental atmosphere and authentic dishes including sushi.

The hotel's recreational facilities include an Executive Fitness Centre located beside the beautiful and extensive garden pool. Guests can also enjoy using the floodlit tennis courts, bowling alley, swimming pools and gymnasium; they can play billiards and snooker or simply test their skill in the video games area. A tennis coach and a masseur are also on hand.

In keeping with its motto, 'Hospitality is our business', the hotel offers quality five-star service.

Safir International Kuwait is managed by Safir International Hotel Management which also looks after several hotels and catering facilities in Kuwait including the Safir Airport Hotel and housekeeping and catering services to the Bayan Palace. Properties abroad include three hotels in Egypt, a Nile cruise and two properties in Syria.

Failaka, the rooftop speciality restaurant, overlooks the city's picturesque coastline.

The SAS Kuwait Hotel, surrounded by a host of palm trees, is centrally located and within easy reach of the airport.

The Royal Club room on the Executive Floor is elegant and functional.

The Peacock Restaurant offers authentic Chinese cuisine from four regions.

SAS KUWAIT HOTEL

A lovely private beach fronts the SAS Kuwait Hotel which lies just 15 minutes from the city's commercial and banking district. Kuwait International Airport is a mere five minutes away and complimentary transfers meet every incoming guest.

Being only a 10-minute drive from the International Fair Ground, the hotel also provides ideal accommodation for international delegates attending exhibitions.

Although its new interiors maintain the Arabic influence of its owners the hotel still retains the ambience of the heritage of the Scandinavian management team and the busy European patronage.

Surrounded by palm trees and an array of first-class sporting facilities, including two swimming pools, three tennis courts, four squash courts and the Nautilus Fitness Centre, the hotel provides visitors with 205 guestrooms in three distinct styles: the Royal Club, Scandinavian and Oriental Rooms and six suites and apartments. Each room is appointed with a 20-channel TV and two movie channels, direct dial telephone, private answering machine, hair dryer and personal safe.

Guests can expect 24-hour room service and express three-hour laundry for clothes collected before 8pm daily.

Dining is a pure delight at the SAS Kuwait Hotel. The Peacock Chinese Restaurant offers authentic Chinese cuisine from the four regions of Shezhuan, Canton, Shanghai and Peking. The Al Boom is a unique hand-built Arabian dhow that has been converted into a Grill Restaurant. It boasts its own Iranian bread oven where freshly baked bread is served to guests. The 'Catch of the Day' has become a favourite with diners.

In keeping with the hotel's relaxed 'resort' style feel, guests can also dine in the Bistretto Restaurant with an Italian atmosphere, step into the Eedam Café for cappucino and cake or laze around the pool soaking up the sun.

The SAS Kuwait Hotel combines up-to-date facilities for the businessman with an informal and casual flavour for an evening of relaxation after business hours.

Right: The Al Boom, a unique hand-built Arabian dhow, has been converted into a Grill Restaurant.
Below: The hotel lobby sports a fascinating centrepiece, the 'kugel', a granite ball that floats on a bed of water.

SHERATON KUWAIT HOTEL AND TOWERS

For most residents and visitors, the Sheraton Kuwait is more than just a hotel. It's a landmark and has a roundabout named after it at a major road intersection in the heart of the city. The Sheraton Kuwait was the first international hotel to open in Kuwait in 1966, and the first Sheraton Hotel to be established outside the United States.

Refurbished in first-class style, after considerable damage during the invasion, renovation is due to be completed by the end of 1993. Three tower blocks sport 304 spacious and comfortable guestrooms and suites, equipped with modern amenities.

The Executive Floor caters exclusively to the needs of the businessman with a well-equipped and extensive Business Centre. The hotel's convenient location in the heart of the commercial centre makes it a popular choice of the busy traveller. It offers an airport limousine service to and from the International Airport, just 15 minutes away. The hotel also undertakes free visa arrangements.

Above: The Sheraton Kuwait Hotel and Towers has a roundabout in the heart of the city named after it.

The hotel's new swimming pool.

Above: Opulence and style in the new elegant lobby.

The Sheraton Kuwait takes great pride in its international cuisine and presents a delectable variety. The Al Hambra Restaurant has à la carte dining and sumptuous buffets. The Persian Restaurant, Shahrayar's, caviar and home-made ice cream are incomparable. And for a fine Italian repast there's Riccardo.

For those who have a weakness for Chinese food, the Chinese Restaurant will prepare selective Cantonese food with Dimsum and Peking Duck specialities. The English Tea Lounge will serve light snacks in a traditionally English setting.

The hotel is also reopening an old-time favourite — Tarbouche, the Lebanese speciality restaurant.

On the sports and leisure front, which is also getting a facelift, the hotel features a modern, fully-equipped health club, a squash court and swimming pool with fresh and natural refreshments, and a poolside snack bar that will make a splash anytime.

The new-look Sheraton Kuwait Hotel and Towers, in its grand and resplendent setting of an age gone by, lives up to its quality service and facilities in all respects.

One of the guestrooms in the hotel.

Below: The Riccardo is one of Kuwait's premier gourmet restaurants.

LOOKING TO THE FUTURE

Few countries in the world have achieved as much as Kuwait, or seen so much change over such a staggeringly short period of time. The people of Kuwait have proved time and again that they are resilient and resourceful, that they love their country and their homeland.

There have been plenty of challenges for the Kuwaiti people over the last 300 years. Perhaps the greatest to date is the need for careful, planned rebuilding of their country, at a time of financial constraints. Kuwait is working to ensure that the events and lessons of the past few years are never forgotten. Vital research is being carried out into the exact environmental effects of the oil spills and fires, so that the whole world learns from Kuwait's suffering. Kuwait is currently operating a deficit budget, and is talking of privatising its service industries; the threat from Iraq has not yet receded fully, and businesses need to be re-established. But the Kuwaiti people proved during the Occupation that they could still work hard to survive, and now that elections have been held there is a positive sense of optimism that the future will see a restoration of the good life.

This is a critical period for Kuwait, one when it must look to the future, and also not neglect the past. Old buildings, the last links with Kuwait's pre-industrial past are crumbling, and Sheikha Hussa stresses that these must be restored and maintained as part of the Kuwaiti heritage.

It is clear that things will never be the same again and that much of what was special in Kuwait has been damaged, maybe even lost. Only the coming decades will tell how much can be restored, and whether Kuwait can rise to this, the most difficult challenge of all.

Kuwait's children: free again to build the future.

The renowned Water Towers, symbols of Kuwait.

Selected Bibliography

Abu Hakima, Ahmad Mustafa: *The Modern History of Kuwait.*

Al Damkhi, Ali: *Invasion — Saddam Hussein's Reign of Terror in Kuwait.*

Al Hammadi, Dr Abdulla: *The Big Terrorism of Nations' Destroyers.*

Dickson, H R P: *The Arab of the Desert.*

Dickson, Violet: *Forty Years in Kuwait.*

Kuwait Ministry of Information: *Kuwait Facts and Figures 1988.*

Kuwait Ministry of Information: *Kuwait Facts and Figures 1992.*

Scarce, Jennifer M: *The Evolving Culture of Kuwait.*

Vine, Peter and Casey, Paula: *Kuwait, A Nation's Story.*

Wells, Suzi and Al Batini, Bazza: *Traditions.*

Acknowledgements

Photography by   Stephanie McGehee
                        Gerry Collis
                        Ministry of Information
                        Gustavo Ferrari
                        Jorge Ferrari
                        Gail Seery

The author wishes to thank the many merchant families of Kuwait who helped in her research for this book.

Special thanks to Stephanie McGehee for her photographs of the damage and destruction after the Occupation, to Kathy McGregor for her tour of the damaged SAS Hotel, and to Malik Kaukab for his help with last-minute photographic requirements.

My thanks also to Paul for his patience, Tareq Al Wazzan for his guidance on the Arabic language, and to all at Motivate Publishing for their help, encouragement and support.

The Author

Gail Seery is a British journalist and writer who has lived and worked in the Middle East for over 12 years. She arrived in Kuwait in 1984, and apart from during the Occupation when she was fortunate to find herself on leave abroad, she has lived there ever since. She has witnessed a surprising degree of change in the country during her residence, and as a journalist, covered events of major national and international significance. Her work has also taken her around the Arabian Gulf region and beyond.

Gail Seery has contributed to numerous publications in Kuwait, throughout the Gulf region, and in the UK and USA. She is well-known in Kuwait for her work with the *Arab Times* newspaper, and especially for her humorous articles. Prior to the invasion she ran her own public relations company specialising in the organisation of promotional events and publicity, primarily in the field of motorsports. During the invasion she was active in organising publicity events on behalf of various Kuwait associations and appeared on television to argue on Kuwait's behalf on a number of occasions.

She developed a keen interest in Kuwait's history and culture, and through her work has conducted a considerable amount of research into the past and present of the country. She contributed a chapter on Kuwait to *Arabian Profiles*, a book in Motivate Publishing's Arabian Heritage Series, and also wrote the *Pocket Guide to Kuwait.* She is currently editor of the *Kuwaiti Digest*, a quarterly magazine published by Kuwait Oil Company.

Gail Seery is married with two children.

INDEX

THE ARABIAN HERITAGE SERIES

Arabian Profiles
edited by Ian Fairservice
and Chuck Grieve

Land of the Emirates
by Shirley Kay

Enchanting Oman
by Shirley Kay

Bahrain – Island Heritage
by Shirley Kay

Kuwait – A New Beginning
by Gail Seery

Dubai – Gateway to the Gulf
edited by Ian Fairservice

Abu Dhabi – Garden City of the Gulf
by Peter Hellyer and Ian Fairservice

Fujairah – An Arabian Jewel
by Peter Hellyer

Portrait of Ras Al Khaimah
by Shirley Kay

Sharjah – Heritage and Progress
by Shirley Kay

Architectural Heritage of the Gulf
by Shirley Kay and Dariush Zandi

Emirates Archaeological Heritage
by Shirley Kay

Seafarers of the Gulf
by Shirley Kay

Gulf Landscapes
by Elizabeth Collas and Andrew Taylor

Birds of Southern Arabia
by Dave Robinson
and Adrian Chapman

Falconry and Birds of Prey in the Gulf
by Dr David Remple and Christian Gross

Mammals of the Southern Gulf
by Christian Gross

The Living Desert
by Marycke Jongbloed

Seashells of Southern Arabia
by Donald and Eloise Bosch

The Living Seas
by Frances Dipper and Tony Woodward

Sketchbook Arabia
by Margaret Henderson

The Thesiger Collection
a catalogue of photographs
by Wilfred Thesiger

Thesiger's Return
by Peter Clark
with photographs by Wilfred Thesiger

Storm Command
by General Sir Peter de la Billière

This Strange Eventful History
by Edward Henderson

Juha – Last of the Errant Knights
by Mustapha Kamal,
translated by Jack Briggs

Fun in the Emirates
by Aisha Bowers
and Leslie P. Engelland

Mother Without a Mask
by Patricia Holton

Premier Editions

Desert, Marsh and Mountain
by Wilfred Thesiger

A Day Above Oman
by John Nowell

Forts of Oman
by Walter Dinteman

Land of the Emirates
by Shirley Kay

Enchanting Oman
by Shirley Kay

Abu Dhabi – Garden City of the Gulf
edited by Ian Fairservice
and Peter Hellyer

Arabian Heritage Guides

Snorkelling and Diving in Oman
by Rod Salm and Robert Baldwin

The Green Guide to the Emirates
by Marycke Jongbloed

Off-Road in the Emirates
by Dariush Zandi

Off-Road in Oman
by Heiner Klein
and Rebecca Brickson

Spoken Arabic – Step-by-Step
by John Kirkbright

Arabian Albums

Dubai – An Arabian Album
by Ronald Codrai

Abu Dhabi – An Arabian Album
by Ronald Codrai

MOTIVATE
PUBLISHING